EMMANUEL JOSEPH

Quiet Confidence: Embracing Your Silent Strength

Copyright © 2025 by Emmanuel Joseph

All rights reserved. No part of this publication may be reproduced, stored or transmitted in any form or by any means, electronic, mechanical, photocopying, recording, scanning, or otherwise without written permission from the publisher. It is illegal to copy this book, post it to a website, or distribute it by any other means without permission.

First edition

This book was professionally typeset on Reedsy.
Find out more at reedsy.com

Contents

1. Chapter 1: The Power of Silence — 1
2. Chapter 2: Embracing Your Inner Introvert — 4
3. Chapter 3: The Strength in Listening — 5
4. Chapter 4: Finding Confidence in Quietness — 6
5. Chapter 5: The Art of Thoughtful Communication — 7
6. Chapter 6: The Benefits of Reflective Practice — 8
7. Chapter 7: Building Resilience Through Inner Strength — 9
8. Chapter 8: The Strength in Vulnerability — 10
9. Chapter 9: The Power of Mindfulness — 11
10. Chapter 10: Cultivating Empathy and Connection — 12
11. Chapter 11: The Importance of Self-Acceptance — 14
12. Chapter 12: Living a Life of Quiet Confidence — 16

1

Chapter 1: The Power of Silence

Introduction

In a world that often celebrates the loudest voices and the most extroverted personalities, quiet confidence can seem like an elusive trait. However, there is a profound strength in those who move through life with a serene and steadfast demeanor. This book, "Quiet Confidence: Embracing Your Silent Strength," aims to illuminate the power of quietness and guide readers on a journey of self-discovery and empowerment.

Quiet confidence is not about being timid or reserved; it is about possessing an inner strength that does not need to be broadcasted to be validated. It is the ability to stand firm in your beliefs and values, even when they go against the grain. This form of confidence allows individuals to navigate the world with grace and resilience, unfazed by external pressures.

Throughout this book, we will explore the many facets of quiet confidence, from the power of silence and active listening to the strength in vulnerability and self-acceptance. We will delve into the unique qualities that introverts bring to the table and how these traits can be harnessed for personal and professional success. By embracing our silent strength, we can unlock our full potential and lead more fulfilling lives.

One of the key aspects of quiet confidence is the power of silence. In a society that often equates loudness with power, the ability to remain silent and composed can be a strategic advantage. Silence allows us to listen more effectively, process information, and respond thoughtfully. It can also serve as a powerful tool in negotiations and decision-making, where measured responses often yield better outcomes.

Active listening is another crucial component of quiet confidence. By truly hearing others and understanding their perspectives, we can build stronger connections and foster trust. This empathetic approach can enhance our personal relationships and professional interactions, making us more effective communicators and leaders.

Embracing our introverted nature can also lead to greater self-awareness and fulfillment. Introverts often have a deep sense of reflection and introspection, which allows them to understand their strengths and weaknesses better. This self-awareness can lead to personal growth and a greater sense of purpose. By valuing these qualities, introverts can thrive in a world that often favors extroverted traits.

Quiet confidence also involves embracing vulnerability. Being open and honest about our feelings and experiences can be a source of strength rather than weakness. By sharing our vulnerabilities, we can build deeper connections with others and foster a sense of trust and empathy. This authenticity can lead to more meaningful and supportive relationships.

Self-acceptance is another pillar of quiet confidence. Recognizing and embracing our true selves, with all our strengths and imperfections, allows us to find inner peace and contentment. This self-acceptance can empower us to pursue our goals with determination and resilience, without being hindered by the need for external validation.

Mindfulness and reflective practice are valuable tools for cultivating quiet confidence. By being present and fully engaged in the moment, we can develop greater self-awareness and emotional intelligence. Reflective practice allows us to learn from our experiences and make better decisions, leading to personal and professional growth.

Finally, quiet confidence is about leading with integrity and authenticity. By staying true to our values and beliefs, we can inspire others and create positive change. This form of leadership fosters trust and respect, making us effective role models in our communities and workplaces.

CHAPTER 1: THE POWER OF SILENCE

As we embark on this journey through "Quiet Confidence: Embracing Your Silent Strength," we will discover the many ways in which silent strength can be harnessed and celebrated. Through introspection, empathy, and authenticity, we can unlock our full potential and lead lives that are both fulfilling and impactful.

In a world where noise often equals power, silence can be seen as a weakness. However, silence holds a different kind of strength, one that is often overlooked. It allows for introspection, providing the space to understand our thoughts and emotions deeply. Embracing silence can lead to a greater sense of self-awareness and inner peace.

Silence also enables us to listen more effectively. When we are quiet, we can truly hear others, leading to stronger connections and more meaningful relationships. This active listening can be a powerful tool in both personal and professional settings, fostering understanding and empathy.

Moreover, silence can be a strategic advantage. In negotiations and discussions, staying silent can often lead to better outcomes. It allows us to process information, think critically, and respond thoughtfully rather than react impulsively. This thoughtful approach can build respect and trust.

Finally, silence can be a source of creativity. In the quiet moments, our minds can wander and explore new ideas without distraction. This creative thinking can lead to innovative solutions and new opportunities, making silence a valuable asset in any endeavor.

2

Chapter 2: Embracing Your Inner Introvert

Introverts often feel pressured to conform to extroverted norms, but there is power in embracing your introverted nature. Introverts tend to be great listeners, which can lead to deeper and more meaningful conversations. This ability to connect on a profound level can strengthen relationships and foster trust.

Introverts also excel in independent work, often producing high-quality results due to their ability to focus deeply. This focus can lead to mastery in their chosen fields, making them valuable assets in any team or organization. Embracing this strength can lead to greater career satisfaction and success.

Moreover, introverts are often reflective, taking the time to think things through before acting. This reflective nature can lead to better decision-making and problem-solving. By embracing this quality, introverts can contribute valuable insights and perspectives that might otherwise be overlooked.

Finally, introverts are often more self-aware, understanding their strengths and weaknesses better than most. This self-awareness can lead to personal growth and a greater sense of fulfillment. Embracing your inner introvert can be a powerful step towards realizing your full potential.

3

Chapter 3: The Strength in Listening

Listening is a skill that is often undervalued in today's fast-paced world. However, it is one of the most powerful tools we have for building connections and understanding others. By truly listening, we can gain deeper insights into the thoughts and feelings of those around us.

Active listening involves not just hearing the words, but also understanding the emotions behind them. This empathetic approach can lead to stronger relationships and a greater sense of trust. It allows us to respond in a way that is supportive and understanding, fostering a sense of connection.

Listening can also be a source of learning. By paying attention to others, we can gain new perspectives and ideas that we might not have considered. This continuous learning can lead to personal and professional growth, making us more adaptable and knowledgeable.

Moreover, listening can be a calming presence in a world full of noise. It allows us to take a step back, process information, and respond thoughtfully. This thoughtful approach can lead to better decision-making and more effective communication, both in our personal and professional lives.

4

Chapter 4: Finding Confidence in Quietness

Q uietness is often mistaken for shyness or lack of confidence, but it can be a source of great strength. Quiet individuals often have a deep sense of self-awareness and inner peace, which can be a powerful foundation for confidence. This quiet confidence can inspire trust and respect in others.

Quietness allows for thoughtful reflection, leading to better decision-making and problem-solving. This thoughtful approach can build confidence in one's abilities and judgment. By embracing quietness, individuals can develop a strong sense of self-assurance and inner strength.

Moreover, quiet individuals often excel in listening and observing, gaining a deeper understanding of the world around them. This understanding can lead to greater empathy and connection with others, building confidence in their ability to navigate social interactions.

Finally, quietness can be a source of resilience. In the face of challenges, quiet individuals can draw on their inner strength and calm demeanor to persevere. This resilience can build confidence and help them overcome obstacles, leading to personal and professional growth.

5

Chapter 5: The Art of Thoughtful Communication

Thoughtful communication is a powerful tool for building connections and fostering understanding. It involves not just speaking, but also listening and responding in a way that is considerate and empathetic. This thoughtful approach can lead to stronger relationships and more effective communication.

Thoughtful communication requires self-awareness and reflection. By taking the time to understand our own thoughts and emotions, we can communicate more clearly and authentically. This authenticity can build trust and respect, making our interactions more meaningful.

Moreover, thoughtful communication involves understanding the needs and perspectives of others. By listening actively and responding with empathy, we can foster a sense of connection and understanding. This empathetic approach can lead to more collaborative and supportive relationships.

Finally, thoughtful communication can lead to better decision-making and problem-solving. By considering different perspectives and responding thoughtfully, we can find more effective solutions and make better choices. This thoughtful approach can lead to greater success in both personal and professional settings.

6

Chapter 6: The Benefits of Reflective Practice

Reflective practice involves taking the time to think deeply about our experiences and actions. This practice can lead to greater self-awareness and personal growth, helping us understand our strengths and weaknesses better. By reflecting on our actions, we can learn from our mistakes and make better choices in the future.

Reflective practice can also lead to improved decision-making and problem-solving. By considering different perspectives and analyzing our experiences, we can find more effective solutions and make better choices. This thoughtful approach can lead to greater success in both personal and professional settings.

Moreover, reflective practice can help us understand our emotions better, leading to greater emotional intelligence. By reflecting on our feelings and reactions, we can develop better coping strategies and build resilience. This emotional intelligence can lead to stronger relationships and a greater sense of well-being.

Finally, reflective practice can be a source of creativity and innovation. By taking the time to think deeply and explore new ideas, we can find innovative solutions and opportunities. This creative thinking can lead to personal and professional growth, making reflective practice a valuable tool for success.

7

Chapter 7: Building Resilience Through Inner Strength

Resilience is the ability to bounce back from challenges and setbacks. It is a key component of success and well-being. Building resilience involves developing inner strength and a positive mindset, allowing us to persevere in the face of adversity.

Inner strength comes from self-awareness and self-acceptance. By understanding our strengths and weaknesses, we can develop a sense of confidence and self-assurance. This inner strength can help us navigate challenges and overcome obstacles.

Moreover, building resilience involves developing a positive mindset. By focusing on our strengths and successes, we can build a sense of optimism and hope. This positive mindset can help us stay motivated and persevere in the face of challenges.

Finally, building resilience involves developing strong support systems. By fostering positive relationships and seeking support when needed, we can build a sense of connection and support. This support can help us navigate challenges and build resilience, leading to greater success and well-being.

8

Chapter 8: The Strength in Vulnerability

Vulnerability is often seen as a weakness, but it can be a source of great strength. By being open and honest about our feelings and experiences, we can build stronger connections and foster trust. This authenticity can lead to more meaningful relationships and a greater sense of connection.

Being vulnerable requires courage and self-acceptance. By embracing our imperfections and being honest about our struggles, we can build a sense of confidence and self-assurance. This authenticity can build trust and respect, making our interactions more meaningful.

Moreover, vulnerability can be a source of growth and learning. By being open to feedback and willing to learn from our mistakes, we can develop greater self-awareness and personal growth. This willingness to learn and grow can lead to greater success and well-being.

Finally, vulnerability can lead to greater empathy and understanding. By being open about our own experiences, we can foster a sense of connection and understanding with others. This empathy can lead to stronger relationships and a greater sense of well-being.

9

Chapter 9: The Power of Mindfulness

Mindfulness is the practice of being present and fully engaged in the moment. It can lead to greater self-awareness and a sense of inner peace. By practicing mindfulness, we can develop a greater sense of self-awareness and emotional intelligence.

Mindfulness can help us manage stress and anxiety. By being present and fully engaged in the moment, we can develop better coping strategies and build resilience. This emotional intelligence can lead to greater well-being and a sense of inner peace.

Moreover, mindfulness can lead to improved decision-making and problem-solving. By being present and fully engaged, we can consider different perspectives and make more thoughtful choices. This thoughtful approach can lead to greater success in both personal and professional settings.

Finally, mindfulness can be a source of creativity and innovation. By being present and fully engaged, we can explore new ideas and find innovative solutions. This creative thinking can lead to personal and professional growth, making mindfulness a valuable tool for success.

10

Chapter 10: Cultivating Empathy and Connection

Empathy is the ability to understand and share the feelings of others. It is a key component of building strong relationships and fostering a sense of connection. By cultivating empathy, we can develop stronger connections and a greater sense of well-being.

Empathy requires active listening and understanding. By truly listening to others and trying to understand their perspectives, we can build a sense of connection and trust. This active listening can lead to more meaningful relationships and a greater sense of well-being.

Moreover, empathy involves being open and honest about our own feelings and experiences Moreover, empathy involves being open and honest about our own feelings and experiences. By sharing our vulnerabilities and listening to others, we can build a deeper sense of trust and connection. This mutual understanding fosters a supportive environment where people feel valued and understood.

Empathy also allows us to navigate conflicts more effectively. By understanding the perspectives and emotions of others, we can find common ground and resolve disputes amicably. This skill is invaluable in both personal relationships and professional settings, leading to stronger and more harmonious interactions.

Practicing empathy can also enhance our leadership abilities. Leaders who are empathetic and understanding are more likely to inspire loyalty and commitment from their teams. By showing genuine concern for the well-being of others, empathetic leaders can create a positive and motivating work environment.

Finally, empathy can lead to a greater sense of fulfillment and happiness. By building strong connections and fostering understanding, we can create a supportive network of relationships. This sense of community and belonging can contribute to our overall well-being and satisfaction in life.

11

Chapter 11: The Importance of Self-Acceptance

Self-acceptance is the foundation of true confidence and inner strength. It involves recognizing and embracing our strengths and weaknesses, and understanding that we are worthy just as we are. This self-awareness can lead to greater peace and contentment.

Embracing self-acceptance allows us to let go of the need for external validation. By valuing ourselves, we can find confidence within, rather than relying on the approval of others. This inner confidence can empower us to pursue our goals and dreams with determination and resilience.

Moreover, self-acceptance encourages us to practice self-compassion. By being kind and forgiving to ourselves, we can build a healthier and more positive relationship with our inner selves. This self-compassion can lead to greater emotional well-being and resilience.

Self-acceptance also involves setting realistic and meaningful goals. By understanding our strengths and limitations, we can set achievable objectives that align with our true selves. This alignment can lead to a greater sense of fulfillment and purpose in our lives.

Finally, self-acceptance can enhance our relationships with others. By being authentic and true to ourselves, we can attract and build connections with people who appreciate us for who we are. This authenticity can lead to more meaningful and lasting relationships.

12

Chapter 12: Living a Life of Quiet Confidence

Living a life of quiet confidence means embracing our inner strength and trusting in our abilities. It involves recognizing the power of silence, reflection, and empathy, and using these qualities to navigate the world with grace and resilience.

Quiet confidence allows us to lead with authenticity and integrity. By staying true to our values and beliefs, we can inspire others and create positive change. This authenticity can build trust and respect, making us effective leaders and role models.

Moreover, living with quiet confidence involves continuous growth and self-improvement. By embracing reflective practice and seeking new learning opportunities, we can develop our skills and abilities. This commitment to growth can lead to greater success and fulfillment in all areas of our lives.

Quiet confidence also means cultivating a positive mindset and resilience. By focusing on our strengths and maintaining a hopeful outlook, we can navigate challenges with grace and determination. This resilience can empower us to overcome obstacles and achieve our goals.

Finally, living a life of quiet confidence involves building strong and supportive relationships. By practicing empathy and active listening, we can foster deeper connections and create a sense of community. This support network can enhance our well-being and contribute to a fulfilling and meaningful life.

Book Description: Quiet Confidence: Embracing Your Silent Strength

In a world that often celebrates the loudest voices and the most extroverted personalities, "Quiet Confidence: Embracing Your Silent Strength" offers a refreshing perspective on the power of silence and introspection. This enlightening book explores the unique qualities that introverts bring to the table and how these traits can be harnessed for personal and professional success.

"Quiet Confidence" delves into the many facets of silent strength, from the power of active listening and thoughtful communication to the strength found in vulnerability and self-acceptance. Readers will discover how embracing their inner introvert can lead to greater self-awareness, emotional intelligence, and a sense of inner peace.

Through a blend of practical advice, reflective exercises, and inspiring stories, this book provides readers with the tools they need to cultivate quiet confidence. It highlights the importance of mindfulness, resilience, and authenticity, guiding readers on a journey of self-discovery and empowerment.

Whether you're an introvert looking to embrace your strengths or an extrovert seeking to understand and appreciate the power of quietness, "Quiet Confidence" offers valuable insights for anyone seeking to lead a more fulfilling and impactful life.

www.ingramcontent.com/pod-product-compliance
Lightning Source LLC
Chambersburg PA
CBHW072023290426
44109CB00018B/2331